Symbols of Freedom

National Parks

Sequoia and Kings Canyon National Parks

Nancy Dickmann

Heinemann Library
Chicago, Illinois

Customer Service 888-454-2279
Visit our website at www.heinemannlibrary.com

Page layout by Ron Kamen and edesign
Photo research by Maria Joannou and Erica Newbery
Illustrations by Martin Sanders
Printed and bound in China by South China Printing Company Limited

10 09 08 07 06
10 9 8 7 6 5 4 3 2 1

Library of Congress Cataloging-in-Publication Data
Dickmann, Nancy.
   Sequoia and Kings Canyon National Parks / Nancy Dickmann.
      p. cm. -- (Symbols of freedom)
   Includes bibliographical references and index.
   ISBN 1-4034-7798-1 (library binding - hardcover)
   1. Sequoia National Park (Calif.)--Juvenile literature. 2. Kings Canyon National Park (Calif.)--Juvenile literature. I. Title. II. Series.
   F868.S4D53 2006
   917.94'82--dc22

                              2005026577

Acknowledgments
The author and publishers are grateful to the following for permission to reproduce copyright material:
Alamy Images pp. **13** (Emmanuel Coupe), **15** (Roberto Soncin Gerometta), **16** (Celeste Daniels); Corbis pp. **5** (Robert Holmes), **7** (Kennan Ward), **8**, **10** (Galen Rowell), **11** (Galen Rowell), **17**, **21** (Galen Rowell), **22** (David Muench); Fotosearch pp. **14**, **20**; Getty Images p. **24** (National Geographic/Norbert Rosing); Hutchison pp. **18** (Eye Ubiquitous), **25** (Eye Ubiquitous); Library of Congress p. **9**; Photolibrary.com p. **4**; Photri pp. **26** (L.NovakHowe), **27** (R.Ginn); Science Photo Library p. **13**

Cover photograph of Sequoia and Kings Canyon National Parks reproduced with permission of Photolibrary.com.

Some words are shown in bold, **like this**. You can find out what they mean by looking in the glossary.

Contents

Our National Parks

National parks are areas of land set aside for people to visit and enjoy **nature**. These parks do not belong to one person. They belong to everyone in the United States.

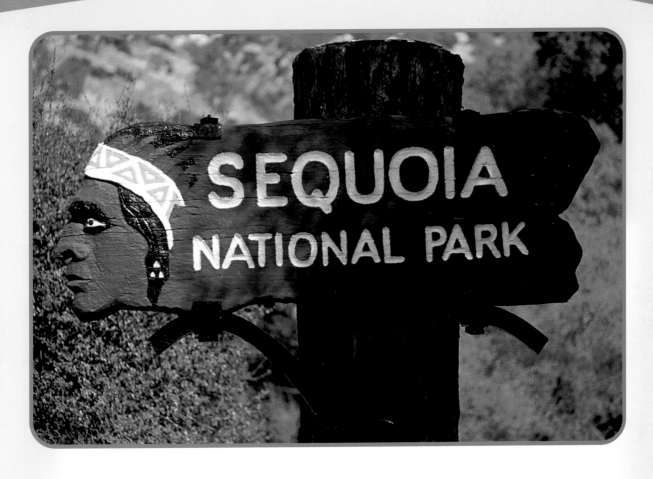

There are **388** national park areas in the
United States. Sequoia and Kings Canyon are
two popular parks. They have some of the
biggest trees in the world.

Sequoia and Kings Canyon National Parks

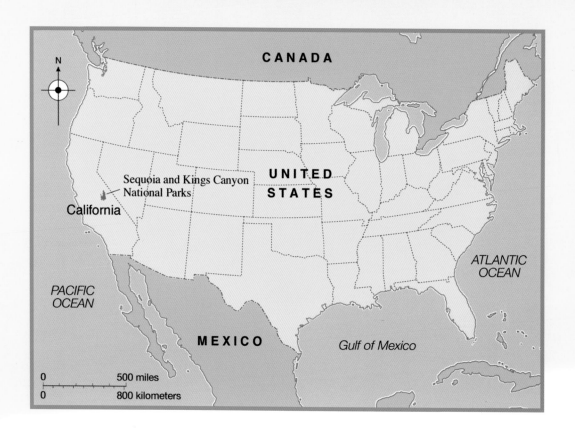

Sequoia and Kings Canyon National Parks are in central California, high in the Sierra Nevada **mountain range**. The parks are separate, but they are run as a single park.

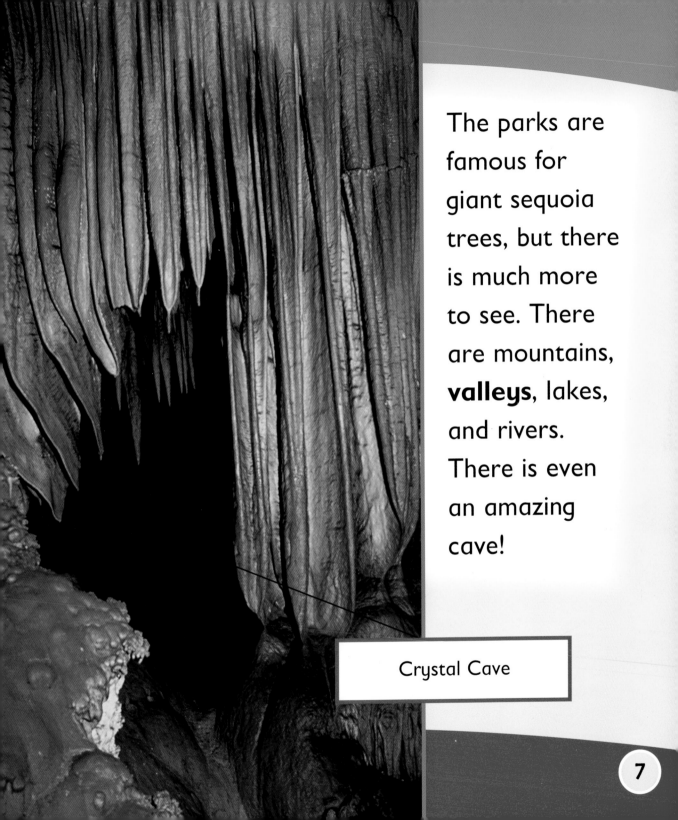

The parks are famous for giant sequoia trees, but there is much more to see. There are mountains, **valleys**, lakes, and rivers. There is even an amazing cave!

Crystal Cave

Sequoia and Kings Canyon Long Ago

For thousands of years, Native Americans lived in the Sequoia and Kings Canyon area. Later, Spanish explorers visited. When gold was discovered in 1848, more people came.

Some people cut down the trees for **lumber**.

John Muir was one of the people who helped protect the trees.

Some people wanted to protect the land. In 1890, Sequoia and General Grant National Parks were created. General Grant became a part of Kings Canyon National Park in 1940.

Visiting Sequoia and Kings Canyon

Many park visitors come in summer, when the weather is warm. They can drive or walk though **groves** of giant sequoia trees. They can also camp, fish, hike, and explore caves.

Some visitors like to try rock climbing.

In the winter, the Sierra Nevada gets a lot of snow. Some of the park roads close. Visitors can still go **snowshoeing** and cross-country skiing on the paths.

Sequoia Trees

Giant sequoia trees are the biggest living things on Earth. They only grow in parts of California. Sequoia and Kings Canyon National Parks have about 30 sequoia **groves**.

A giant sequoia tree can be as tall as a 30-story building.

Giant sequoia trees are very tough.
Their thick bark protects them from fire,
insects, and disease. A giant sequoia tree
can live for more than 3,000 years!

Huge trees will grow from
the tiny seeds in these
giant sequoia cones.

Giant Forest

One of the largest sequoia **groves** is "Giant Forest." The General Sherman Tree is found here. It is the biggest living thing in the world.

The General Sherman is named after a famous general from the **Civil War**.

There are many smaller plants. Ferns grow on the forest floor, among the giant sequoias. In spring, fields of wildflowers can be found in many places.

Mountains, Valleys, and Canyons

Mount Whitney is the tallest mountain in the lower 48 states.

The Sierra Nevada **mountain range** runs through the two parks. Its most famous peak is Mount Whitney. Many visitors climb to the top of Moro Rock to enjoy the view.

Deep **valleys** are found between the mountains. There are also **canyons** that were worn away by rivers. Some of these canyons are deeper than the Grand Canyon!

Rivers and Lakes

The Kings River begins high in the mountains and flows down into the flatter areas. In spring, the mountain snow melts. The river flows fast and wild.

South Fork of Kings River

There are also more than 2,600 lakes and ponds in Sequoia National Park alone! Many visitors enjoy fishing in the lakes.

Park Animals

Foxes, bobcats, and snakes live in the **foothills** of the parks. Mountain lions and bighorn sheep live higher in the mountains. Sierran black bears live throughout the parks.

Visitors must not try to feed or pet any animals in the park.

yellow-bellied marmot

Many marmots are found in Mineral King Valley. These large **rodents** are known for climbing into the engines of visitors' cars. They like to chew on engine hoses.

visitor center

There are three visitor centers in Sequoia and Kings Canyon National Parks that are open all year. Visitors can get information about the parks there.

Park rangers work in the visitor centers and in other places around the parks. Rangers lead hikes and give talks about the **wildlife** of the parks.

Map of Sequoia and Kings Canyon

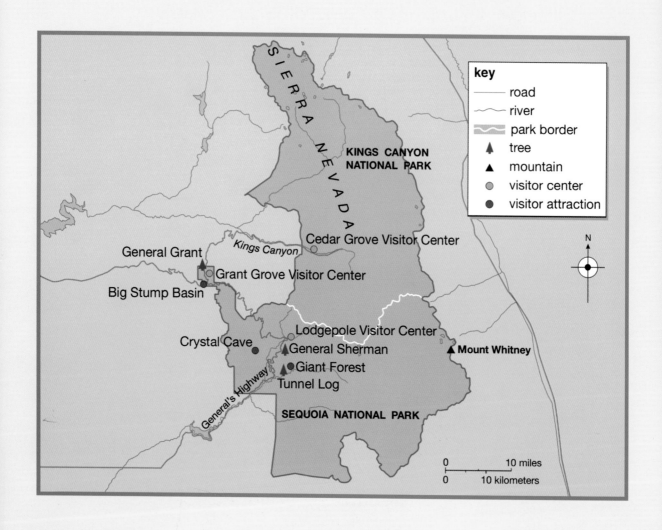

SIERRA NEVADA

KINGS CANYON
NATIONAL PARK

key
— road
～ river
▨▨ park border
▲ tree
▲ mountain
● visitor center
● visitor attraction

Cedar Grove Visitor Center

General Grant

Kings Canyon

Grant Grove Visitor Center

Big Stump Basin

Lodgepole Visitor Center

Crystal Cave

General Sherman

Mount Whitney

Giant Forest

Tunnel Log

General's Highway

SEQUOIA NATIONAL PARK

N

0   10 miles
0   10 kilometers

Timeline

about 2,100 years ago	The General Sherman Tree starts growing.
about 1,700 years ago	The General Grant Tree starts growing.
1848	Gold is discovered in California.
1890	Sequoia National Park becomes the nation's second **national park**.
1903	The "General's Highway," leading to the Giant Forest, is completed.
1926	Sequoia National Park is expanded. The General Grant Tree is named the "Nation's Christmas Tree."
1940	Kings Canyon National Park is created. It includes General Grant National Park.
1943	Sequoia and Kings Canyon begin to be run as a single park.
1965	The Cedar Grove area and the Tehipite Valley are added to Kings Canyon National Park.
1978	The Mineral King area is added to Sequoia National Park.

Glossary

canyon very steep valley

Civil War war between the northern and southern states, from 1861 to 1865

foothill small hill at the foot of a mountain

grove group of trees growing together

logging camp place where trees are cut down for their wood

lumber trees cut down so the wood can be used

mountain range long row of mountains

national park natural area set aside by the government for people to visit

nature the outdoors and the wild plants and animals found there

park ranger person who works in a national park and shares information about the wildlife and unusual sights of the park

rodent animal with special front teeth for gnawing

snowshoe to travel on top of the snow on snowshoes that are attached to boots

valley low area between hills or mountains

wildlife wild animals of an area

Find Out More

Books

An older reader can help you with these books:

Domeniconi, David. *M is for Majestic: A National Parks Alphabet.* Farmington Hills, Mich.: Gale Group, 2003.

Galko, Francine. *Mountain Animals.* Chicago: Heinemann Library, 2003.

Mader, Jan. *Rocky Mountains.* San Francisco: Children's Press, 2004.

Royston, Angela. *Mountains.* Chicago: Heinemann Library, 2005.

Address

To find out more about Sequoia and Kings Canyon National Parks, write to:

Sequoia and Kings Canyon National Parks
47050 Generals Highway
Three Rivers, CA 93271-9700

Website

You can visit the parks' official website at:
http://www.nps.gov/seki

Index